GLIMPSES OF THE KING

A STUDY OF MATTHEW

BIBLE STUDIES TO IMPACT THE LIVES OF ORDINARY PEOPLE

Written by Dorothy Russell

The Word Worldwide

CHRISTIAN FOCUS

For details of our titles visit us on our website
www.christianfocus.com

ISBN 1-84550-007-5

Copyright © WEC International

Published in 2004 by
Christian Focus Publications Ltd, Geanies House,
Fearn, Tain, Ross-shire, IV20 ITW, Scotland
and
WEC International, Bulstrode, Oxford Road,
Gerrards Cross, Bucks, SL9 8SZ

Cover design by Alister MacInnes

Printed and bound by Bell & Bain, Glasgow

CONTENTS

PREFACE 4

INTRODUCTORY STUDY.. 5

QUESTIONS AND NOTES

STUDY 1 – THE KING GETS READY 7

STUDY 2 – LIVE LIKE A KING 11

STUDY 3 – THE KING'S POWER FLASHES FORTH... 14

STUDY 4 – MARCHING ORDERS FOR THE KING'S SUBJECTS 18

STUDY 5 – SECRETS OF THE KINGDOM 21

STUDY 6 – THE GREAT ONES IN THE KINGDOM.. 25

STUDY 7 – VALUES OF THE KINGDOM 29

STUDY 8 – THE KING COMES TO JERUSALEM 33

STUDY 9 – THE KING TELLS WHAT WILL HAPPEN 37

STUDY 10 – IS THIS MAN A KING? 41

STUDY 11 – THE KING TRIUMPHS 45

ANSWER GUIDE

STUDY 1 51

STUDY 2 52

STUDY 3 53

STUDY 4 54

STUDY 5 55

STUDY 6 56

STUDY 7 57

STUDY 8 58

STUDY 9 59

STUDY 10 60

STUDY 11 61

PREFACE

GEARED FOR GROWTH

'Where there's LIFE there's GROWTH:
Where there's GROWTH there's LIFE.'

WHY GROW a study group?

Because as we study the Bible and share together we can

- learn to combat loneliness, depression, staleness, frustration, and other problems
- get to understand and love each other
- become responsive to the Holy Spirit's dealing and obedient to God's Word

and that's GROWTH.

How do you GROW a study group?

- Just start by asking a friend to join you and then aim at expanding your group.
- Study the set portions daily (they are brief and easy: no catches).
- Meet once a week to discuss what you find.
- Befriend others, both Christians and non-Christians, and work away together

see how it GROWS!

WHEN you GROW ...

This will happen at school, at home, at work, at play, in your youth group, your student fellowship, women's meetings, mid-week meetings, churches and communities,

you'll be REACHING THROUGH TEACHING

INTRODUCTORY STUDY

INTRODUCING THE KING – WHO IS HE? 30+ 24 (' (16.

Why are there four Gospels? Wouldn't it have been better to have one complete biography of Jesus? Why do they leave out so much of his life?

Interesting questions! Perhaps the answer could be summed up by saying that each of the four Gospel writers wrote to bring out a different theme.

Matthew, a Jew, shows us Jesus as KING, the One who fulfilled the Jewish prophecies in the Old Testament.

Mark paints a portrait of Jesus as the Divine SERVANT.

Luke, a Gentile, highlights the perfect Man, SAVIOUR of the whole world.

John glories in Jesus as the earthly manifestation of the ETERNAL GOD. He states his purpose in writing: 'that you may believe that Jesus is the Messiah, the Son of God, and that through your faith in Him, you may have life' (John 20:31, GNB).

This study is designed to highlight the way Matthew shows us – JESUS THE KING.

This does not aim to be a comprehensive study on the whole of Matthew's Gospel, so you will notice that passages are selected for study each week. You will also find it helpful, though not essential, to read the intervening verses as you do the questions at home.

✽ ✽ ✽

What first comes to your mind when you hear the word 'King'? Discuss your thoughts.

What is the usual way for a person to become a king?

How is this different from a President or Prime Minister?

So, the first question Matthew answers is – Where did He come from? Who were His Ancestors?

Look through Matthew I verses I-17 and pick out any names you are familiar with.

Who is at the top of the family tree? Who is the first king mentioned?

Read verse I6 carefully. How does Matthew make it clear that this is Jesus' legal, but not physical pedigree?

Read aloud chapter I:18–2:18. As you do, be aware that Matthew writes this section in order to explain chapter I verse I6. The most important thing in the first two chapters of Matthew is the genealogy – He is at pains to point out Jesus' royal line of ancestry and to prove that Jesus was not the illegitimate son of some unknown father, or even the natural son of Joseph. Matthew records the true facts, which have become so familiar to us.

* * *

NOW LET'S GET IT STRAIGHT!
Close your Bibles and do the following Quiz:

1. Does Matthew tell us the men from the East were kings?
2. What kings are mentioned in the story?
3. Did the wise men follow the star from the East to Jerusalem?
4. How many wise men were there?
5. Did they find the baby in the stable?
6. Are we given their names?

This account in Matthew's Gospel is the only record in the Bible of the visit of the wise men (astrologers) so any 'embroidery' which appears on our Christmas cards has been added since!

A few thoughts:
The motive of the wise men was worship.
The motive of King Herod was destruction of a possible rival.
When you recognize Jesus as King of Kings, do you want to worship Him? Or do you reject His Kingly claim on your life?
If you leave Him out of daily life, you are rejecting His Kingship.

Someone has said: 'Wise men seek Jesus still.'

STUDY 1 *(7ᵗʰ FEB)*

THE KING GETS READY

QUESTIONS

DAY I *Matthew 3:I, II-14; John I:23-27.*
a) What did John the Baptist know about the coming Messiah, or King, at this stage?

Marea

b) Why do you think John said what he did in verse 14? (I Pet. 2:22 and I John 3:5).

DAY 2 *Matthew 3:I5.*

Mani

a) There are two significant reasons why Jesus offered Himself for baptism. Try to discover the first one by using 2 Corinthians 5:21 (Good News Bible especially good) to help you.

b) Baptism is a symbolic action. It symbolises death to sin and death to self. Be prepared to discuss the second reason with your group, by thinking over Romans 6:3, 4.

DAY 3 *Matthew 3:I6, I7.*
a) Refer to Acts I0:38 to find out what God was doing here.

BIRa

b) What parts do the three persons of the Trinity – Father, Son and Holy Spirit – play in this drama?

DAY 4 *Leviticus I2:6, 8; Luke 2:22-24.*
a) What was the Jewish significance of the dove?

Me

QUESTIONS (contd.)

b) Can you see any link between the thoughts of Day 2, and God's 'coronation' of His Son?

DAY 5 *Matthew 4:1-7. How did Jesus answer the devil?*
(a) 'Since you are superior to the rest of mankind, why go hungry? Satisfy your physical needs – You are God, You can give the orders!'

Adrian

(b) 'OK. You have declared your trust in God. Now put Him to the test. See if He is really trustworthy.'

DAY 6 *Matthew 4:8-11. How did Jesus answer the devil?*
a) 'You are ready to begin your life's work which God has sent you to do. I can give you instant success if you bow down and worship me.'

Jean

b) What happened next? (v. 11).

DAY 7 a) Jesus had many choices to make in preparation for His life's work. Can you summarise those you have discovered in this weeks study?

Brian

b) When you have an important choice to make, what do you do? How can Hebrews 4:15, 16 help you?

NOTES

The coronation of Her Majesty Queen Elizabeth II of Britain was a splendid affair. Colour and pageantry, coaches and glittering crowns, gave a fairy-tale quality to the occasion. There was one part of the ceremony, however, which stood out in stark contrast to the rest.

As Handel's music flooded the Abbey, the Queen's jewellery and robes were lifted off her, piece by piece, by her Maids of Honour. Her ceremonial train was taken by the Groom of the Robes, and Elizabeth II stood, divested of all her finery, ready for her consecration.

Enthroned in King Edward's chair and clothed symbolically in a simple sleeveless overdress of plain white linen, Elizabeth received the tokens of her responsibility – the Orb, the Sceptre, the Rod of Mercy, and the royal ring of England.

Then came the moment of the crowning itself. Elizabeth bowed her head, and slowly and solemnly the crown descended upon her.

* * *

Jesus clothed Himself with humility as He went down into the waters of baptism. Then, coming up out of the water, He was crowned with the power of the Holy Spirit by Almighty God the Father.

Let's consider:

THE KING IN RELATION TO MANKIND

If Jesus had merely come to earth to be a perfect example for man to follow, then it would have been a farce for Him to offer Himself for John's baptism. John preached a message of repentance, but Jesus had no sin to repent of. So we must look deeper into this story.

By His action Jesus was proclaiming –

a) His identification with sinners, so that He might put away sin and bring men into His Kingdom.
b) His willingness to die to His own will and to accept the will of the Father and death on the cross.

THE KING IN RELATION TO GOD THE FATHER

His coronation was immediate. God anointed Him with the Holy Spirit – with power to accomplish that Divine will, the way of the cross.

Psalm 2 reads: 'I have installed my King on Zion, my holy hill. You are my Son.'
So spoke the Voice from heaven, and added: '... with Him I am well pleased.'

THE KING IN RELATION TO THE UNDERWORLD OF EVIL

The King has come! Yes, but there is a usurper on the throne, who will fight to retain it. The encounter comes to Jesus at a time of physical weakness and the sword is thrust at the three most vulnerable areas of man's life:

> The physical – Bodily desires
> The spiritual – Trust in God.
> His life's work and purpose – Responsibility.

How does Jesus meet these cleverly planned attacks?

1. Even His bodily needs are subject to the Father's word. He chooses rather to deny Himself the necessities of life, than to act independently of His Father.
2. His trust in God is so complete that He has no need to put Him to the test. If He had done this it would have been an admission that He harboured an element of doubt.
3. He has already accepted the Father's will for His life, and nothing will turn Him from it. Jesus knew there was only one way to gain the kingdoms of this world, through suffering and dying.

So the King is ready, prepared and strengthened for His ministry ... and His atoning death. 'The Son of God appeared for this very reason,' He was to say later, 'to destroy what the devil had done.'

STUDY 2
LIVE LIKE A KING

QUESTIONS

DAY 1 *Matthew 4:23–5:2; 9:36.*
a) Describe the 'crowds' whom Jesus was so concerned about.

Mu

Matthew 5:1, 2.
b) To whom did Jesus address the teachings that followed?

c) So, who are these instructions for today?

DAY 2 *THOUGHT ATTITUDES Matthew 5:3-6*
Compare the first half of verse 3 with Matthew 18:3, 4.
Compare the first half of verse 4 with 2 Corinthians 7:10.

B'Ra Compare the first half of verse 5 with Matthew 11:29.
Compare the first half of verse 6 with John 7:37-39.
a) What are the four characteristics referred to here?

b) Work out why these are essential for entry into the Kingdom.

DAY 3 *THOUGHT ATTITUDES Matthew 5:7-9.*
a) The first parts of these verses show Christ-like characteristics
Marea which will develop in the life of a believer. What are they?

Matthew 5:10-12.
b) When we are persecuted, for what reason can we be glad?

DAY 4 *BLESSINGS Matthew 5:3-12.*
a) From these verses, list the blessings we can enjoy from God as we
Mani develop Christian character.

QUESTIONS (contd.)

b) Would you say happiness comes as a result of our circumstances, or because of our relationship with God?

DAY 5 *THOUGHT POISONS. Pick out the dangerous attitudes of mind that can poison our characters, and ruin our witness for the Lord:*

Key verses	Thought poisons	Further reading
Matthew 5:21, 22		vv. 21-26
Matthew 5:27, 28		vv. 27-32
Matthew 5:34, 37		vv. 33-37
Matthew 5:38, 39		vv. 38-42
Matthew 5:43, 44		vv. 43-48

DAY 6 *THOUGHT POISONS. Do the same as yesterday.*

Key verses	Thought poisons	Further reading
Matthew 6:1		vv. 1-18
Matthew 6:19, 20		vv. 19-24
Matthew 6:25		vv. 25-34
Matthew 7:1, 2		vv. 1-15

Consider the lists you have made yesterday and today. Talk to the Lord about each one, and let Him show you where you need to ask forgiveness.

DAY 7 *Matthew 7:24-29.*
a) Who is the wise man in the story like?

b) In order to 'Live like a King', do you have to have something, do something, or be something? In other words is it your possessions, your conduct, or your character that is the most important?

c) Look up the word 'manifesto' in a dictionary. It has been said that the chapters we have studied this week are the manifesto of the King. Do you agree?

NOTES

'Live like a king!' said the advertisement. It was a tourist brochure encouraging people to spend a holiday in a castle in Ireland.

But this week's study has shown us how we can live like the King of Kings, if we allow Him to work in our lives.

* * *

'Seeing the crowds....' Jesus' heart yearned over the people of the world. He saw their desperate needs, which could only be met by making Him King in their individual lives. Until they did this, they would not be able to appreciate or obey the King's law.

What does 'the world' today think of the ideals expressed in these chapters – turning the other cheek, loving your enemies? It laughs at them. 'How unrealistic!' they say. 'Fancy turning the other cheek, when the fellow needs a good kick in the pants!'

So Jesus gathered His disciples around Him and explained to them the kind of Kingdom He wanted to build in the lives of His followers. The law of the Kingdom is given to those:

> who love Jesus
> who are loyal to Him
> and who want to obey Him

It is an inner law, for those who have given their inner selves to the King. Jeremiah prophesied about the Lord's people: 'The Lord declares, "I will put my law in their minds, and write it on their hearts"' (Jer. 31:33).

So it is the Lord who enables His followers to keep His law, and they can then become salt and light in the world, thus bringing 'the crowds' into the kingdom, by their witness.

Remember. It is quite impossible to take 'the Sermon on the Mount' (as this passage has been called) and demand that men obey it, if they have not submitted themselves to the King. Every blessing that Jesus promises is a blessing for those who are in the Kingdom, not outside it.

STUDY 3
THE KING'S POWER FLASHES FORTH

QUESTIONS

DAY 1 *Read Matthew 9:35-38 aloud, then Matthew 8:1-10, 13.*
a) What did the man with leprosy and the Roman official have in common when they came to Jesus? (vv. 2, 8).

b) How can the requests of these two men help us when we come to Jesus, praying for ourselves or others?

DAY 2 *Read Matthew 9:35-38 aloud, then Matthew 8:14-17.*
a) How did Jesus heal this woman?

b) What did He do as a fulfilment of Isaiah's prophecy?

DAY 3 *Read Matthew 9:35-38 aloud, then Matthew 8:23-27 and Psalm 89:8, 9.*
a) To whom did Jesus show His power in this story?

b) What did they learn about their Master that day?

c) How can this story help you in your daily life?

DAY 4 *Read Matthew 9:35-38 aloud, then Matthew 8:28-34.*
a) How is it made clear in this story that Jesus was dealing with the demons, not the men?

QUESTIONS (contd.)

In Mark's gospel we have an even more vivid description of this happening. Read Mark 5:1-20.

DAY 5 *Read Matthew 9:35-38 aloud, then Matthew 9:18. This incident is told more fully in Luke 5:17-26.*
a) Discuss what the paralysed man might have been thinking at the various stages of the story.

b) What did he learn about Jesus' character and authority?

DAY 6 *Read Matthew 9:35-38 aloud, then Matthew 9:18-26.*
a) What difference can you find between the two people who came to Jesus for help?

b) How was this little girl's raising to life different from Jesus' resurrection on Easter Day?

DAY 7 *How much of Matthew 9:35-38 can you remember? Matthew 9:27-34.*
a) Jesus asked the blind men a question. How is this echoed in some of the other stories, e.g., 8:10, 26; 9:2, 22?

b) What were some of the reactions to these demonstrations of Jesus' power? See 8:19, 34; 9:3, 8, 33, 34.

NOTES

Look at the King! See Him going through the towns and villages teaching, preaching, and healing every kind of disease. We can see with our eyes the results of His miraculous power in healing diseases – yet there is nothing theatrical about His mighty acts. They are natural, beautiful, performed to meet each individual at his point of need.

Why didn't Jesus set up as a doctor? Think of the many more He could have healed if He had done this full-time. Well, why didn't He?

Look at Him again. He demonstrates His power over:

leprosy – in the Old Testament the symbol of sin.
paralysis, fever, blindness – suffering is the result of sin in the world.
demon possession – the very agents of sin.
sin itself – 'Your sins are forgiven'.
death – which comes to every man because of sin.

The mission of the King was supremely to deal with SIN.

Can you see, in each instance we have considered this week, how Jesus was dealing at more than a surface level with each case? He was going deeper, to the root of the problem. So today, when we come to Him with a need – be it physical or emotional – let us remember to allow Him to probe into our very souls, and exercise His power over anything He wants to put right in us.

Andrew Murray writes:

'Above all, God would draw us into closer fellowship with Himself. We learn to realize that the *fellowship* and *nearness* and *love* of God are more to us than the answers to our petitions; and we continue in prayer.'

* * *

We have seen that faith was vital to the experiencing of Jesus' restoring power.

The faith of an outcast, the scum of society: 'If you are willing, you can make me clean.'

The faith of a Gentile (outside God's covenant) and a Roman, at that: 'Just say the word and my servant will be healed.'

The faith of a woman, second-class citizen, and unclean: 'If only I touch His cloak, I will be healed.'

The faith of two, with no physical vision, only spiritual: 'Do you believe?' 'Yes!' These people received blessing.

In contrast, there were all the inhabitants of a certain town who saw His wonderful works and went out to meet Him – and what did they do? They pleaded with Him to go away.

He did.

Doesn't this say something to you?

Meditate on the wonderful truth behind the quaint words of John Newton's hymn:

> Come, my soul thy suit prepare,
> Jesus loves to answer prayer,
> He Himself has bid thee pray,
> Therefore will not say thee nay.
>
> Thou art coming to a King,
> Large petitions with thee bring,
> For His grace and power are such
> None can ever ask too much.

STUDY 4 21ˢᵗ Mar

MARCHING ORDERS FOR THE KING'S SUBJECTS

QUESTIONS

DAY 1   *Matthew 9:35-38; 10:1-4.*
a) Put in your own words the burden which was on Jesus' heart at this time.

Me ·

b) What did Jesus tell the disciples to do in 9:38 and what did He do Himself (10:1)?

DAY 2   *Matthew 10:5-15.*
Jesus gives instructions to these twelve men who are beginning their ministry. What He says will apply throughout their lives and the lives of their successors – even to us.
a) To whom were they to go?

alison .

b) What were they to say?

c) What were they to do?

d) What were they to take?

e) Would they be well received?

DAY 3   *Matthew 10:16-23; 28:19, 20.*
a) Was it dangerous to go where Jesus told them to go?

Marea

b) What kind of treatment were they to expect?

QUESTIONS (contd.)

c) Who would enable them to speak? (Matt 10:20).

DAY 4 *Matthew 10:24-31.*
a) With whom are God's servants to identify? (v. 25).

B'Ra

b) Who is the only one we are to fear? (v. 28).

c) For what purpose does the Church exist? (v. 27).

d) How are Christians to encourage themselves? (v. 29-31).

DAY 5 *Matthew 10:32-42*
a) What can you find that would be a comfort or an encouragement to those who put Christ and His work first in their lives?

Jean.

b) Can you give an example of verse 39?

DAY 6 *Matthew 12:1-8.*
a) Summarise the answer Jesus gave to the Pharisees' criticism in verse 2.

Marie

b) What two startling claims did Jesus make about Himself? (vv. 6, 8). Think how these claims would have shocked the Pharisees.

DAY 7 *Matthew 12:9-14.*
a) Why did Jesus tell the story about the sheep in verse 11?

Belair/

b) Look back to yesterday's answers as well as today's and discuss what so enraged the Pharisees.

NOTES

Campbell Morgan writes:

'As the King stood in the midst of the twelve, He looked at them and the immediate present; but He also looked with those clear, far-seeing eyes into the near decades; and He looked still further down the centuries. Then, speaking to the first apostles, He delivered a charge which, in its comprehensiveness and finality, is applicable to the whole movement of His enterprise, until His second advent.'

These marching orders are given to *disciples*, i.e. followers and apprentices of Jesus who seek to learn from him and serve Him.

Disciples are called to share the concern of Jesus for a lost world and to pray for workers to reach them. In turn they are called to answer their own prayers and are equipped to be sent out to fulfil God's purposes.

They were told, *'Go to the lost sheep of the house of Israel'*. In those days it was to the Jewish people only but it implies that God sends His servants to specific people groups seeking to bring them into the Kingdom of God. They are to preach and demonstrate the good news that God reigns, sharing with those who are willing to hear and warning those who are not. They are not to be concerned with their support, for the Lord knows all their needs.

In all things they are to *'be wise'*. This means recognizing that they will be opposed by people who wish to destroy them and their message. They are not to be afraid for the Holy Spirit will enable them to answer their opponents. At the same time they are not to take unnecessary risks, but to move out of dangerous situations so as to be able to minister the gospel elsewhere.

They are expected *to be treated as Jesus was treated*. He was reviled and so will his servants be. The gospel, because of its radical nature, brings division between people, yet in the midst of it all, some will respond and receive the message of life.

STUDY 5

SECRETS OF THE KINGDOM   4ᵗ April.

QUESTIONS

DAY 1   *Matthew 13:1-3, 10-17.*
a) Who did Jesus mean by 'you' and 'them' in verse 11?

B'Ra

b) What was the essential difference between these two types of people? (See also John 1:11, 12).

c) Have you ever heard something, but only realized its full implication later on? Does this help you to understand why Jesus spoke in parables? (See notes).

DAY 2   *Matthew 13:3-9, 18-23.*
a) What were the four responses to the Word of God?

Sean.

b) How many different end results are there? What are they?

c) What does the story say to you personally?

DAY 3   *Matthew 13:24-30, 36-43.*
a) What two things are we told about the field in this parable?

Moreer

b) What does the good seed represent?

c) What can you find out about the devil and his activity?

QUESTIONS (contd.)

DAY 4 *Matthew 13:31-35.*
a) What two things does Jesus say the Kingdom of Heaven is like in these verses? What is common to both?

Alison /.

b) Share some thoughts of how the Kingdom can grow in your town or area.

DAY 5 *Matthew 13:44-46.*
a) What did both men in these parables have to do, in order to get the thing they wanted?

Mari .

b) What does that tell us about the treasure, and the pearl?

c) Can you work out what message Jesus was getting across by these stories?

DAY 6 *Matthew 13:47-50.*
a) Which of the parables we have read this week does this one remind you of?

Me .

b) Why?

c) Discuss the relevance of these two stories to us today.

DAY 7 *Matthew 13:51-53.*
a) Why were the disciples (see v. 36) able to understand Jesus' teaching?

Brian-

b) How can you get the most out of your Bible Study or a sermon in church?

NOTES

What is a parable? Literally, a placing of things side by side (like 'parallel') with the suggestion of a comparison.

An old definition is: 'An earthly story with a heavenly meaning.' Or we could say, a picture of things we can see, intended to reveal and explain things that are unseen.

Please remember that Jesus spoke in parables to help men understand spiritual truths, not to hinder their understanding. It might seem from a superficial reading of verses 10-17 that Jesus wants to withhold the truth from unbelievers. This is not so. It was because of their attitude – rejection of Him – that they could not see the spiritual truth of the stories.

Because they 'had not' (faith in Him), any hope of understanding about the Kingdom was also denied to them. So Jesus told them stories to win their interest and draw them closer to an attitude of acceptance of Himself.

But those who 'had' (faith in Him) were given even more spiritual food, which increased their faith.

Are you a 'have' or a 'have not'?

Are you learning from these parables some basic truths about the Kingdom of Heaven?

✱ ✱ ✱

Let's consider what each story tells about the Kingdom.

	MAIN POINT	KINGDOM SECRET
Sower	Where the seed fell.	Two main results from hearing God's word.
Weeds	Wheat and weeds growing together till harvest.	The end of the age will reveal two types of people.
Net	Net gathers good and bad fish.	
Mustard Seed	Growth from a tiny seed.	The Kingdom of God will grow and spread.
Yeast	Small amount of yeast gives growth.	
Treasure	Each man sold all he had to buy it.	Belonging to the Kingdom is more important than anything else.
Pearl		

It is interesting to notice that the Kingdom of Heaven is portrayed as an inner happening. We cannot see God working in people's hearts, but He is working, nonetheless.

The good seed was hidden in the ground.
The wheat began to grow secretly.
The net was deep in the sea.
The mustard seed was almost unnoticeable.
The yeast was hidden in the dough.
The treasure and the pearl had to be found.

And the end result is all-important. Salvation is the most precious thing we can have in life. The personal surrender to God, and acknowledgment of His Son Jesus Christ as King, gives us an entirely new quality of life here and now. This enables us, like the disciples, to understand His word, and live by it daily.

So Jesus spoke in parables. Perhaps we have heard these stories many times without understanding how they apply to us. We can do what the disciples did – we can come to our Lord and say to Him, 'Help me to understand what this parable means for me.' He will gladly reveal the secrets of His Kingdom.

Lloyd John Ogilvie, in his book *'Autobiography of God'* writes:

'God's conversation with us always gets back to the same subject – the Kingdom of God, and His rule and reign in our hearts.'

THE GREAT ONES IN THE KINGDOM

QUESTIONS

DAY I *Mark 9:33-35; Luke 9:46.* ?. ~~MATTHEW 18 V1-5~~.
a) What were the disciples anxious about? (See Matt. 20:20, 21).

Me

b) Write down the names of four people who are considered great today.

DAY 2 *Matthew 18:1-5.*
a) What characteristics of a little child do you think Jesus meant were necessary for entry into the Kingdom?

B'Ra

b) What did Jesus tell His disciples they would have to do in order to become like little children?

\

DAY 3 Commentators suggest that Jesus, in speaking of 'these little ones who believe in Me' seems to pass from the actual child, to think of weak and immature believers.

Mani

Matthew 18:6-9; 1 Corinthians 8:9.
a) How do these verses in Matthew show both Jesus' infinite tenderness and also His fierce wrath?

b) Think of some way you might be a stumbling block to another Christian, and pray that the Lord will prevent you from committing this sin.

DAY 4   *Matthew 18:10-14 (The note for DAY 3 also applies here).*
a) What kind of people does the world look down on or despise?

Brian

b) How does Jesus illustrate the value of each individual and His concern for their eternal salvation?

DAY 5   *Matthew 18:15-20.*
a) What is the purpose of a Christian obeying verse 15?

Mani

b) Are Jesus' instructions in verses 15-17 practical today?

c) Do you know of any instance where they have been carried out?

DAY 6   *Matthew 18:21-22; Matthew 6:14, 15.*
a) Can you think of someone who has wronged you, spoken against you, or who irritates you time and time again?

Alison

b) In the light of these verses, what should your attitude be?

DAY 7   *Matthew 18:23-35. Note carefully verse 35.*
a) If you belong to the Kingdom of Heaven, you are in the position of the servant in verse 27. Can you see why?

Jean.

b) Would you ever behave in the way this servant did?

NOTES

In chapter 17 Matthew tells us about the time when three of Jesus' disciples were privileged to be with Him on the mountain, and to witness His glory in a unique way. They saw a change come over their Master – His face shone like the sun, and His clothes became dazzling white. What a magnificent vision of their King was given to them!

As things returned to normal and Jesus and His three close friends came down the mountain, they joined the other disciples and made their way to Capernaum.

Can you imagine what the disciples would have talked about as they walked along? Would the other nine have questioned Peter, James and John eagerly about their experience on the mountain? Would they have been thrilled to hear about the supernatural things they had witnessed?

Let's eavesdrop!

Luke 9:46. An argument started among the disciples as to which of them would be the greatest.

Mark 9:33. When He (Jesus) was in the house, He asked them, 'What were you arguing about on the road?' But they kept quiet, because on the way they had argued about who would be the greatest.

Matthew, however, reports that the question was too explosive for them to bottle up, so they blurted out – 'Which of us will be the greatest in the Kingdom of Heaven?'

Morris Inch in his book, *'Celebrating Jesus as Lord',* fills in some detail:

'Jesus looked around at His disciples. They could feel His eyes penetrating their defences as if to find out the most likely candidate. Where would His gaze rest? Whom would He promote? Still Jesus' eyes swept on, past Peter, John, James, away from the inner circle to Thomas, Philip and the remainder. At last, after what must have seemed an eternity, Jesus beckoned to a fragile little figure, a child.

'The Master did not speak until the youngster stood beside Him. 'Whoever then humbles himself as this child' Jesus observed, 'he is the greatest in the kingdom of heaven'. A moment before, the disciples had been pressing close to gain the Lord's favour. They must have resembled a crowd of people waiting impatiently for a sale to begin, jostling for position at the expense of someone else. Now they stood planted to the spot, as if held back by an invisible shield, a shield of their own ambitious making, and now called to their attention by Jesus.'

The parable in verses 23-35 is one of the most disturbing stories Jesus ever told. We are in debt to God because of sin. As the Anglican Prayer Book puts it –

'We have erred and strayed from Thy ways like lost sheep.
We have followed too much the devices of our own hearts,
We have offended against Thy holy laws,
We have left undone those things that we ought to have done,
and we have done those things we ought not to have done.'

But Jesus Christ came to pay that debt! He died that we might be forgiven – freely forgiven by His mercy alone, not by anything we can do.

So we can go forth with our heads held high ... and this parable says to us, 'BEWARE! Now you must forgive others in the same way as God has forgiven you - because you are merciful, not because of anything the other person will do.'

This is not an optional extra, it is a 'must' for the servant of the King.

So .... who are the 'great ones' in the Kingdom? Those who are humble, and those who forgive, and don't hold grudges.

STUDY 7

VALUES OF THE KINGDOM

QUESTIONS

DAY 1 *Matthew 19:1, 2; 20:17-19, 29-34.*
Look at a map and trace the pathway of the King at this time.
a) What was on His mind?

Marea

b) Yet, in spite of pressure, how did He feel towards people in need?

DAY 2 *Matthew 19:3-12; Matthew 5:31-32.*
a) What basic principle about the sanctity of marriage did Jesus
Maini give?

b) Is this still valid today?

DAY 3 *Matthew 19:13-15; Mark 10:14.*
a) Why was Jesus angry?

alison .

b) Why should His disciples have known better?

c) What did Jesus mean by, 'The kingdom of heaven belongs to such as these'?

DAY 4 *Matthew 19:16-24; Mark 10:21.*
a) What did Jesus see was this young man's real problem?

Me

QUESTIONS (contd.)

b) Yet how did He feel towards him?

c) Discuss the lessons the disciples learned from this episode.

DAY 5 *Matthew 19:25-30; Ephesians 2:8, 9.*
a) Look at the disciples' first question. What was Jesus answer?

Bill Rea

b) What reward did Jesus, as King, promise His disciples?

DAY 6 *Matthew 20:1-16; Romans 9:14, 15.*
a) What can we learn about God (the landowner) from this parable?

Brian

b) What are some thoughts that come to your mind as you read this story?

DAY 7 *Matthew 20:20-28; 23:11, 12.*
a) What can we discover about 'Mrs Zebedee' from her request?

Jean

b) What great principle does Jesus again bring to our notice?

c) How can this be worked out practically in our lives today?

NOTES

We can imagine Jesus and His friends, with a crowd following, making their way from Galilee in the north to Judea, crossing the river Jordan to visit the east bank, then returning to go to Jerusalem via Jericho. Wouldn't it have been great to be among that crowd? Matthew was there and he acts as our eyes and ears as he tells us snippets of the conversations that he heard. It might have gone something like this:

Pharisees:	Is it lawful for a man to divorce his wife?
Jesus:	What God has joined together, let not man separate.
Pharisees:	Then why did Moses allow divorce?
Jesus:	Because people were hardened and sinful and could not maintain God's ideal.
Disciples:	(*To the crowd*) Keep those children away from the Master! He's much too busy to bother about them.
Jesus:	Peter! James! Never stop children coming to Me. Let them come. People in my Kingdom must be like these little ones.
Young Man:	Good Master, I have kept the commandments. What else must I do to get eternal life?
Jesus:	Only one more thing, dear friend, Sell all you have and follow Me.
Young Man:	Sell all I have? But that is asking too much.
Jesus:	(*To disciples*) It is very hard for a rich man to enter the Kingdom.
Disciples:	Well then, who can be saved?
Jesus:	Salvation depends on God alone.
Disciples:	We have left everything to follow You. What will be our reward?
Jesus:	You will have rewards in heaven. But remember, many who are first will be last, and many who are last will be first. Listen! I'll show you what I mean. It is not the length of service for Me that earns you a reward, it is your faithfulness in the task when your opportunity comes.
Mrs Zebedee:	Excuse me, Rabbi. Please can you make sure that my two sons, James and John, get important places in your Kingdom?
Jesus:	God, the Sovereign Lord, will choose whom He will.
Disciples:	Listen to her! Why should James and John always get the best perks?
Jesus:	Children of the Kingdom, stop quarrelling! Don't you understand yet? If you want to be great in My Kingdom, you must be a servant to all. If you want to be first, you must put yourself last.

Perhaps the most tantalizing part of this week's study is the parable of the workers in the vineyard. Remember that we cannot push the illustration too far – Jesus was not advocating equal pay for unequal work!

Many people see in this parable the lesson that Christ gives the same gift, eternal life, to all who turn to Him, no matter whether they are in the freshness of youth with all their lives ahead of them, in middle age, or in the eventide of life.

But Campbell Morgan writes:

'The whole application of this parable is to service and the reward of service for men in the Kingdom... This parable is intended to teach one simple truth, that a man's reward will be, not according to the length of his service... but according to his fidelity to the opportunity which is given him.'

'... here is a man to whom is given the opportunity to speak to thousands upon thousands of people the great word of God. It is a great opportunity. But here is a woman living away off upon the mountain, who never saw a city in her life, but who has wrought with God in the training of two or three children. When that man and woman stand for final reward, they will each have their penny if they have been faithful.'

STUDY 8

THE KING COMES TO JERUSALEM

QUESTIONS

DAY 1 *Matthew 21:1-11; Psalm 118:19-29 (A psalm particularly used at the Passover feast).*
a) What can you find out about the crowds that followed Jesus?

Jean

b) And the people of Jerusalem?

c) Discuss the possible reasons why Jesus entered Jerusalem in this way at this time (See also Matt. 20:18, 19; Zech. 9:9).

DAY 2 *Matthew 21:12-17.* Picture the scene described in these verses.
a) Who is the central figure? What is He doing? Why?

P) Ra

b) Who came into the temple while the place was in chaos?

c) What were the children doing?

DAY 3 *Matthew 21:23-27.*
a) What do the questions the priests and elders asked show about themselves?

Marea

b) Why do you think Jesus refused to give them a straight answer? (See John 7:17).

QUESTIONS (contd.)

DAY 4   *Matthew 21:28-32.*
a) In Jesus' explanation of this parable, who were like the first son? Why?

Marri

b) Who were like the second? Why?

DAY 5   *Matthew 21:33-46; Isaiah 5:1, 2, 7.*
a) In the Bible, the 'vineyard' always symbolizes the same thing. What is it?

Alison

b) Can you identify the owner; the tenants; the owner's servants; and the owner's son?

DAY 6   *Matthew 21:33-46 (read the same verses as yesterday).*
a) Can you see yourself as one of God's 'tenants'?

Me

b) What has He entrusted you with: your body? your children? your money? your career? your talents? responsibility in your church?

Think this over and see if you have refused to acknowledge the Lord's ownership in any of these areas.

DAY 7   *Matthew 22:1-14.* It has been suggested that verses 2 and 3 represent the time of Christ's earthly ministry.

Brian   a) How did those who were invited respond?

QUESTIONS (contd.)

b) Verses 4-7 look forward to the period of the early church, ending with the destruction of Jerusalem in AD 70. What were two reactions of that time?

c) Verses 8-14 look forward to the gathering of the Gentiles. How are we shown that God still requires holiness of character? (See Isa. 61:10. Good News Bible is not helpful here).

NOTES

Behold your King is coming!
This is the official entry of the Son of God into the city of God!
This King who rides in triumph, Who is he?
A carpenter from an obscure village up north.
What kind of kingly robes is he wearing?
A simple home-made garment, hand-woven without a seam.
What trusty steed does he ride?
A beast of burden, a donkey not yet broken to harness.
His courtiers, who are they?
A mob from despised Galilee, some of them uneducated fishermen.
What decorations festoon the streets?
Broken branches and old clothes.

What a contrast to the pomp and pageantry of a Roman Emperor entering the city, riding in State, fresh from his triumphs in battle! Who cares if this Galilean peasant wants to pretend he's a king? The Roman legions of occupation weren't impressed. The authorities weren't worried. And yet...

No procession that ever passed through the streets of Imperial Rome has been remembered so vividly down through the centuries, as this Triumphal Entry of King Jesus into Jerusalem that day. Jerusalem! City of the great King!

The very place that should have recognized and accepted her King, rejects Him and nails Him to a cross. And notice this important point: Because the people of Jerusalem rejected the King, the King was forced to reject the people of Jerusalem.

Listen to the chief priests, teachers of the law and elders of the people: 'Do you hear what these children are saying? Stop them!' 'By what authority are you doing these things? Who gave you this authority?'

And when they heard the parable of the vineyard, they knew He was talking about them. They looked for a way to arrest Him. They went out and laid plans to trap Him in His words.

All through this week's study we have seen Jesus challenging the Jewish leaders, showing them that He knew what was in their hearts. He knew that, in spite of their heritage and privileges, they were rejecting the King and His Kingdom.

Perhaps there are people you know who think they will get to heaven because they are morally good. Pray for an opportunity to share with them the fact that God has prepared only one way to heaven, and that is through His Son. Our own righteousness is never enough, we must put on the righteousness of Christ, and if we want to enjoy the banquet, we must quite deliberately accept the invitation:

'Come unto me ... and I will give you rest.'

STUDY 9

THE KING TELLS WHAT WILL HAPPEN

QUESTIONS

DAY 1 *Matthew 23:37-39; 24:1-5, 23-26.*
Look at the disciples' question in 24:3. Also Mark 13:1, 2.
a) What were the three things they wanted to know?

B'Ra

(They probably assumed all three would happen at the same time).

b) What solemn warning did Jesus give them before answering their question? It applies to us also.

DAY 2 *Matthew 24:6-22.*
a) List some of the things Jesus said would happen before 'the end' would come (vv. 6-14).

Marea

Verses 15-22 speak of the destruction of Jerusalem and its Temple, which came to pass in AD 70.
b) Pick out verses from yesterday's reading which also foretell this.

DAY 3 *Matthew 24:27-44.*
Read again verses 27, 36 and 42.
a) What was Jesus' answer to the disciples question (v. 3), 'What will

Jean

be the sign of your coming?'

b) How does this make you feel?

It would seem, therefore, that verses 32-34 refer to what He has said in verses 15-23, that the destruction of Jerusalem would be heralded by certain signs, to warn believers. Write out verse 35 and learn it.

QUESTIONS (contd.)

DAY 4 *Matthew 24:45-51; Ephesians 2:19.*
a) What were the duties of the servant left in charge? (v. 45). See how this bears out Matthew 20:27.

Brian

b) If the household in this parable stands for the Church, how can each one of us be like the faithful and wise servant?

DAY 5 *Matthew 25:1-13.*
a) The emphasis here is on the individual's relationship with the Lord.

Me

How did the wise virgins differ from the foolish?

b) What is the warning here for us?

DAY 6 *Matthew 25:14-30.*
a) Pick out the things this parable has in common with the ones we have read in the past two days.

auson

b) For what were the first two servants, in this parable, commended? (Compare this with the end of the Notes on Study 7).

DAY 7 *Matthew 25:31-46.*
a) Along with this reading, meditate on the following verses prayerfully, and take time to listen to what God is saying to you: Matthew 16:27; Acts 10:42, 43; Hebrews 9:27, 28.

Main

b) Write down at least one thought to share with your group.

NOTES

Jesus knew He had only two more days to live (26:2). What would you do with your last few precious hours, if you knew you had only two more days to live?

The darkness was closing in around the Light of the world.

* Satan's schemes were coming to a head,
* The Pharisees were plotting His death,
* Judas had already decided to sell his Master,
* The chief priests were watching and waiting for their opportunity.

He had come to His own people, but they had not received Him.

The judgment for this would fall on Jerusalem before very long, and His loving heart was intensely saddened at the thought. 'O Jerusalem, Jerusalem Your house will be left desolate.'

Oh that it might have been otherwise! We can imagine Jesus standing by the beautiful Temple, His heart breaking...

'But Master,' say the disciples, 'come and look at these buildings. They are fine and strong and glorious; they will last forever.'

'No,' replies Jesus, 'not one stone will be left on another; every one will be thrown down.'

His disciples are silent. Together they walk out of the city, down the hill, across the brook, and up the Mount of Olives. Jesus sits down and they look back at the magnificent view of Jerusalem across the valley.

'Tell us Master,' says one, breaking the heavy silence, 'tell us, when this will happen? And what sign will there be? And when is the end of the age before you set up your Kingdom?'

It all happened so naturally. It was the perfect opportunity for Jesus to pass on to His closest friends details of what was going to happen in the future.

I. The Fall of Jerusalem

We know that this happened in AD 70, about forty years after Jesus gave this prophecy. The historical account of the massacre of the Jews and the razing to the ground of the city, including its Temple, makes chilling reading. Try to get hold of a book which tells about this. You will see what Jesus meant by 'distress, unequalled from the beginning of the world until now' (Matt. 24:21).

We also know that the believers heeded the words of Jesus (24:16-18) and literally fled to the mountains without waiting to take any of their possessions, and, those who did so, escaped the siege.

2. The coming of the Son of Man

The King with dignity and assurance, was looking through the darkness of His imminent crucifixion, and past the horror of the destruction of Jerusalem, to the time when the Son of Man would come in His glory.

It hasn't happened yet. We are living in the times before the end, and just as surely as the other prophecies have come true, so will this certainly happen one day, maybe very soon. Nobody knows when Jesus will return, and we are not to be deceived by false prophets who set a date for the end of the world.

One thing is certain, He will come again.

The urgent message which Jesus gave His disciples, and to all His people down through the ages – and therefore to us is – 'You also must be READY, because the Son of Man will come at an hour when you do not expect Him'.

Are you ready? Ready if He should come today?

STUDY 10

IS THIS MAN A KING?

QUESTIONS

This week we look into the hearts of different people connected with the events leading up to the crucifixion (Matt. 26; 27:1-31).

DAY 1 *Matthew 26:6-13; John 12:2, 3.*
a) How did Mary show her love for Jesus? Consider what this action would have meant to Jesus at this time.

Maini.

b) How can we?

DAY 2 *Matthew 26:14-16, 20-25, 47-50.*
a) What did Judas do which showed he was not loyal to Jesus?

Marea

b) Now read Matthew 27:3-5. What changed Judas' attitude?

DAY 3 *Matthew 26:31-46, 50-54, 69-75; John 18:10.*
a) How did Peter feel towards Jesus?

also

b) On what occasions did he fail?

c) Why do you think he failed?

QUESTIONS (contd.)

DAY 4   *Matthew 26:3-5; 57-68.*
a) What was Caiaphas trying to do?

Jean

b) What does this tell you?

c) He asked Jesus a question and got a straight answer. Why did he not believe Him? (vv. 63, 64).

DAY 5   *Matthew 27:1, 2, 11-26.*
a) What was the first question Pilate asked Jesus?

Brian

b) What indications can you find to show that he knew what he ought to do, but didn't do it?

DAY 6   *Matthew 27:27-31.*
a) Why did the soldiers mock Jesus in this manner?

B'Ra.

b) What impression do you get of Jesus throughout His trial?

DAY 7   *Matthew 26:1, 2, 18, 23, 24, 26-31, 53-56.*
a) How did His knowledge of the Scriptures help Jesus at this time?

Mel,

b) How can knowing our Bibles be a help to us?

NOTES

The people we have been looking at are actors in a drama planned by God.

Never forget that Jesus laid down His life of His own accord. No-one took His life from Him. Peter told the Jewish crowds at Pentecost, 'This man was handed over to you by God's set purpose and foreknowledge; and you, with the help of wicked men, put Him to death by nailing Him to the cross.'

As the house lights dim and the curtain goes up, we see Jesus the King, majestically in control of the situation, in the centre of the stage. Other actors have their cues, and come into the spotlight when and how the producer has planned. God, the Producer, has also written the script.

Mary of Bethany
Did she realize that the shadow of the cross lay heavily upon her Master just then? It would seem from Jesus' words that she did. She had grasped what the disciples had so far missed, and she showed her love and devotion in the best way she could. The fragrance and the warmth of her action light up the whole scene for us.

Judas
He flits across the stage, always in the half-light – going to the chief priests in secret, pretending love for his Master, hoping he would not be found out, identifying Jesus in the dark with a traitor's kiss, and finally, in guilt and desperation, committing suicide.

Peter
His changes of mood compel our attention – could it be that we see ourselves in this man?

- Engagingly self-confident and loyal: 'I will never run away.'
- Willing to watch and pray, but discovering his weakness.
- Acting on impulse in a crisis, rebuked by the Master.
- Wanting to stay close to Jesus, but falling victim to the most devastating failure of his life.

Weeping bitter tears of repentance, and not even realizing that he can be forgiven.

Caiaphas
Who is the villain of the plot? Judas? Caiaphas? Pilate?

Determined and coldly calculating, Caiaphas makes his plans. Jesus must go. It can easily be arranged. But not until Passover is finished and the crowds have gone (See how God's plan differed here!). Here's an informer. Good. Give him whatever he wants, and get the job done. OK, OK, even if it has to be during the Feast.

And here is the scene Caiaphas has been waiting for. The Prisoner is standing before him. He has Him just where he wants Him. Dear me! He says He is God – well that's it. It was quite simple after all, wasn't it?

Pilate

Of all the actors, this one has the most striking costume. Rome dressed its governors to look dignified and proud. All the power and authority of the Empire were behind Pilate – but as he acts his part, we are amazed! Through the brash, pompous exterior we see a weak man, unsure of himself, making half-hearted gestures to evade the responsibility of condemning his Prisoner, whose presence radiated calmness and strength of character. History remembers only his guilt. Thousand of lips have affirmed, 'Jesus suffered under Pontius Pilate....'

The Soldiers

They had been there, of course, to provide the backing for the main characters in the drama. To them it was all in a day's work, the chance of a bit of fun, nothing to take seriously. Rather amusing really – 'He says He's a King? Well, let's give Him a robe and a crown!'

* * *

In Stainer's magnificent cantata, *'The Crucifixion'*, one aria is entitled 'The Majesty of the Divine Humiliation.' The tenor soloist sings:

'Not in Thy Majesty, robed in Heaven's supremest splendour,
But in weakness and surrender, Thou hangest here.
Who can be like Thee?
Pilate, high in Zion dwelling? Rome, with arms the world compelling?
Proud though they be, Thou art sublime!
Here, in abasement, crownless, poor, disrobed and bleeding –
Thou art the King! Thou art the King!'

* * *

Is He a King?

That question could have been put to each of these people, and their answers would have served, not to decide the character of Jesus, but to indicate the character of each one who replied.

Jesus is Lord! Jesus is King!

How do you respond to this? Your response will not alter the fact that He is King, but it will decide your eternal destiny.

STUDY 11

THE KING TRIUMPHS

QUESTIONS

DAY 1 *Matthew 27:32-37, 41, 42.*
a) What was the charge laid against Jesus, for which He received the death sentence?

Me.

b) How did the religious leaders make use of this?

DAY 2 *Matthew 27:37-44.*
The account of our Lord's agony and the onlookers' mockery raises the question, 'Why did God not intervene?'
B'ea a) What would the chief priests have answered?

b) What would you answer?

DAY 3 *Matthew 27:45-53.*
God the Father was not disinterested however.
Marea What supernatural events happened at the time of the crucifixion?

Read and meditate on 2 Corinthians 5:21 and Hebrews 12:2.

DAY 4 *Matthew 27:54-66.*
Some people try to explain away the resurrection by saying that Jesus did not really die. He merely swooned.
Sean a) List the different people recorded here who knew for certain that He was dead.

QUESTIONS (contd.)

b) Why did the chief priests seal the tomb and put men to guard it?

DAY 5 *Matthew 28:1-10; Revelation 1:18.*
Another earthquake!
a) What effect did the angel have on the guards?

b) What message did the risen Jesus give the women?

DAY 6 *Matthew 28:11-20.*
a) Why would the made-up story in verse 13 never be able to be proved?

b) The 'Great Commission' of Jesus in verses 19 and 20 has never been altered. What do you draw from it for your own personal life?

DAY 7 Spend some time thinking back over the ways in which Matthew has shown us Jesus as King. Then read these verses, think about them, and worship the One who is King over all kings – Philippians 2:9-11; 1 Timothy 1:17; Revelation 19:11-16.

NOTES

'O make me understand it,
Help me to take it in,
What it meant for Thee, the Holy One,
To take away my sin' (K. A. M. Kelly).

The King Triumphs

What was the moment of triumph? It was that moment when the King became our Saviour, crying 'It is finished!' He drew his last earthly breath, and gave up His spirit.

For this He had been born: 'Christ Jesus came into the world to save sinners' (I Tim. 1:15). In this moment His victory over Satan was complete: 'The reason the Son of God appeared was to destroy the devil's work' (I John 3:8).

Bishop Ryle, in his *'Expository Thoughts on the Gospels'* writes,

'There never was a last breath drawn of such deep import as this; there never was an event on which so much depended. That death discharged in full the mighty debt which sinners owe to God, and threw open the door of life to every believer.

That death solved the hard problem, how God could be perfectly holy, and yet perfectly merciful. It opened to the world a fountain for all sin and uncleanness. It was a complete victory over Satan, and spoiled him openly. Never, in fact, was there, or could there be again, such a death. No wonder that the earth quaked when Jesus died in our stead on the accursed tree.'

The Proof of His Triumph

'The King is dead. Long live the King!' could be applied here – but the same King who was dead, is now alive for evermore. God raised Him from death, and thus put His seal on Christ's sacrifice for sin.

If He had not risen, how could we believe He had power over death?

How could we be sure He had paid the ransom for our sin?

How could we know that He is alive, strengthening and guiding us?

Paul says, 'And if Christ has not been raised, your faith is futile, you are still in your sins... But Christ has indeed been raised from the dead...' (I Cor. 15:17-20).

Praise the Lord! The Resurrection of Christ is one of the best attested facts of history. Our faith stands on a solid foundation.

The King's Command

Let us widen our horizons and see the all-embracing vision that Jesus gave to His followers.

ALL authority in heaven and earth has been given to the King.

ALL nations are to be reached with the gospel.

ALL His commands are to be taught to others.

ALWAYS He will be with His subjects.

ANSWER GUIDE

The following pages contain an Answer Guide. It is recommended that answers to the questions be attempted before turning to this guide. It is only a guide and the answers given should not be treated as exhaustive.

GUIDE TO INTRODUCTORY STUDY

Before you hand out the studies –
  Bring along a couple of biographies (which you can lend out later) and talk about them. Then remark that the author must have known the person well, or done a lot of research, so that he could write the book.
  So – let's look at the author of this book first, and see how well he knew his subject. (N.B. Matthew's Gospel is not a biography, as we shall see).
  Invite suggestions from the group on what they know about Matthew and build up a picture. Draw out the following –

* He was a Jew living in Jerusalem.
* He would have attended a synagogue school (boys only).
* He took a job with the hated army of occupation (Matt. 9:9).
* He was one of the Twelve (Matt. 10:3).
* Jesus personally called him to follow Him (Matt. 9:9-10).
* His other name, and his father's name (Mark 2:14).
* He witnessed to his friends (Luke 5:27-32).
* He was wealthy, but left everything.
* Events in common with the other disciples, as far as Pentecost.
* He was inspired to write this Gospel.

Now look at the Introductory pages of the studies together. Be sure you know the answers to the Quiz, and can read out the appropriate verses as answers.

* * *

For your personal meditation (**Leaders**).

The very first thing Matthew does is to show Jesus as son of Abraham (founder of the Jewish race) and son of David (Israel's greatest King). Each of these men was promised a son by God.

ISAAC proved to be a disappointment, in the weakness of his character, and the failure of his descendants to become true 'sons of Abraham'.

JESUS, Son of Abraham by descent, brought many sons to glory.

SOLOMON, though he built the temple, ended his life in dismal failure.

JESUS, Son of David by descent, began building the eternal Temple which will never be destroyed.

It is difficult for us to realize how important it was for the Jews to know Jesus' ancestry. Matthew presents this clearly. Then, having traced the line of Joseph, the legal husband of Jesus' mother, he must show that Jesus is in a unique way, Son of God (Matt. 1:18-21).

Campbell Morgan writes:

'Jesus was connected with a race which could not produce Him. He came into it, was of it, yet distinct from it.'

The Roman senate in 40 BC gave Herod (The Great) the title, 'King of the Jews' and he governed Judea until his death in AD 4. Matthew brings out the contrast between this ruthless king, and the kingship of Jesus, 'a ruler who will be the Shepherd of Israel' (Matt. 2:6). He also shows that Gentiles (the wise men) acknowledged Jesus as 'King of the Jews'.

A worthwhile addition to your study time each week:

Look out some well-known hymns and choruses which speak of Jesus as King.

Each week introduce a verse of one of them, and read it thoughtfully to your group. You might like to write out the words so that they can sing it as well.

Here are some suggestions – you can add some more:

O worship the King.
The Lord is King, lift up your voice.
Let all the world in every corner sing, 'My God and King'.
Praise, my soul, the King of heaven.
Praise to the Lord, the Almighty, the King of Creation.
Crown Him with many crowns.
All hail, King Jesus.
Majesty, worship His Majesty.
Lift up your heads to the coming King.
Reign, King Jesus, reign.
He is Lord.

GUIDE TO STUDY 1

DAY 1 a) He knew that the Messiah would be coming soon, and that he, John, was to prepare the way for Him. The Messiah would be great and powerful, and John felt quite unworthy even to be His servant. He would baptise with the Holy Spirit and with fire.
b) He must have been inspired by God to say this, and it must have been revealed to him that here was the Sinless Son of God.

DAY 2 a) He wanted to identify with mankind, to share our sin, so that we might share His righteousness.
b) Jesus' act of baptism foreshadowed His death on the cross (Luke 12:50). By it, He declared His willingness to die for the sin of the world. It also served as an illustration of how we can identify with Him in His death.

DAY 3 a) Although Jesus was filled with the Spirit from His conception, God was now anointing Him for His ministry – with the Holy Spirit and power.
b) The Father spoke from Heaven, the Son received the commendation, the Holy Spirit rested on Him.

DAY 4 a) A dove was used as a sin-offering which even the poorest could afford.
b) By submitting to baptism, Jesus showed His willingness to obey God's plan for man's salvation; and because of this, God said, 'I am well pleased with Him.'

DAY 5 a) It is written: 'Man does not live on bread alone, but on every word that comes from the mouth of God.'
b) It is written: 'Do not put the Lord your God to the test.'

DAY 6 a) It is written: 'Worship only the Lord your God.'
b) Angels came and ministered to Him.

DAY 7 a) He had to decide if He would:
   – be baptised or not.
   – commit Himself to God's plan for His life.
   – satisfy His physical desires before God permitted it.
   – prove that He really could trust God.
   – win the world by a way that did not include the cross.
b) Jesus knows what it is like to have to make difficult decisions, and we can confidently come to Him for help.

MATTHEW • ANSWER GUIDE • • • • •

51

GUIDE TO STUDY 2

DAY 1   a) Sick people needing healing. People who were worried and helpless, like sheep without a shepherd.
b) To His disciples.
c) They are for believers and we cannot expect unbelievers to appreciate or obey them.

DAY 2   a) Humility; repentance; meekness; a desire for Jesus.
b) To come into the Kingdom we need to admit our need, repent of sin, and ask Christ into our lives.

DAY 3   a) Mercy; purity of heart; the art of making peace. Only God can produce these qualities in our lives.
b) Because of our faith in Christ.

DAY 4   a) Belonging to the Kingdom as sons of God: comfort; future glory; satisfaction; mercy; seeing God; reward in heaven.
b) Personal (these verses indicate the latter).

DAY 5   Anger; lust; swearing; revenge; hate.

DAY 6   Boasting; greed; worry; criticism.

DAY 7   a) The wise man represents the person who hears the words of Jesus and puts them into practice.
b) Character.
c) Personal.

GUIDE TO STUDY 3

DAY 1
a) They both believed that Jesus could work the miracle of healing.
b) We, too, can affirm our faith in His healing power.

DAY 2
a) He touched her hand.
b) He drove out spirits and healed all who were sick.

DAY 3
a) His disciples.
b) That He was perfectly composed, even in a crisis; that he had sympathy for them; authority over nature; and that He was Someone far greater than they had realized.
c) Personal.

DAY 4
The words are those of the demons; Jesus clearly sent them into the pigs, and we are told the effect this had on the pigs.

DAY 5
a) When there was no room – disappointment.
   When the friends told him their plan – hope.
   On the floor at Jesus feet – wonder and warmth.
   His sins forgiven – deep peace.
   Healing – wonderful joy.
b) That He went to the root of the problem, his sin, and had authority to deal with that.

DAY 6

a) Rich man	Poor woman
Asked for his daughter	Asked for herself
Had joy for 12 years	Had sorrow for 12 years
Came openly	Came secretly
Had to wait till they got home	Healed instantly
Child raised from death	Healed of bleeding

b) The girl presumably died again later in life but Jesus became alive – forever.

DAY 7
a) Jesus frequently commented on the faith of the people who came to Him.
b) Some wanted to follow Him and praised God; others rejected Him and accused Him of blasphemy and demon-possession.

MATTHEW • ANSWER GUIDE . . . .

GUIDE TO STUDY 4

DAY 1
a) His burden was for the lost, who thought they were saved, but in fact were not.
b) Ask (pray) that God would send in workers; He called the twelve apostles. (**Leaders**, point out: As we ask God for people to do His work, He may well say to us, 'You do it').

DAY 2
a) They were to go to those that were lost, those who needed to hear the message about the Kingdom of God.
b) 'The Kingdom of heaven is near.'
c) Meet the needs of the people on all levels, as God has met theirs.
d) Nothing, trusting God to meet all their needs.
e) No. Some would welcome them, others would reject them.

DAY 3
a) Yes and no! The people were described as 'wolves', but Jesus was with them.
b) Opposition and persecution of all sorts.
c) The Holy Spirit.

DAY 4
a) The Lord Jesus.
b) God.
c) Proclaiming the message of Jesus.
d) In the fact that our Father cares for us.

DAY 5
a) That God will reward those who obey Him, and Jesus will acknowledge them before His father.
b) Personal.

DAY 6
a) The great ones in the Jewish religion can waive the laws when necessary – and I am greater than them.
b) I am greater than the Temple; I am Lord of the Sabbath. (These two things were most sacred to the Jews).

DAY 7
a) To show that if an animal can be rescued on the Sabbath, then a man, worth more than an animal, can be healed.
b) The things He claimed for Himself could only be true of God, therefore He claimed to be God.

GUIDE TO STUDY 5

DAY 1
a) The disciples, and the crowd.
b) The disciples had accepted Him, the crowd had not.
c) See Notes for answer.

DAY 2
a) 1. The Word is immediately forgotten.
2. It is received with joy, but put aside when trouble comes.
3. It is received, but soon forgotten among the worries of life.
4. The Word is heard, understood, and acted upon.
b) Two. Hearing and obeying, or not living by it.
c) Personal.

DAY 3
a) The field belonged to a man who sowed good seed in it, while an enemy sowed weeds in it.
b) Christians (Sons of the Kingdom).
c) He works secretly, he is the enemy of God, his work will come to nothing.

DAY 4
a) A mustard seed and yeast. Both are small to begin with but grow.
b) Personal.

DAY 5
a) They had to sell everything they had.
b) They were more precious than anything else.
c) It is more important for a person to accept Christ and come into His Kingdom than anything else in the world.

DAY 6
a) The wheat and the weeds. Because all were together and looked the same until the day when the good and the bad were separated.
b) In our world there are believers and unbelievers and often they seem alike. God knows the difference. The day of reckoning for those who don't belong to Christ is a certainty, and will be terrible beyond our imagining.
c) We should be most concerned for any we know who are outside of Christ.

DAY 7
a) Because they accepted His teachings and were willing to obey (see DAY 1).
b) Come with an open heart and mind, ask the Holy Spirit to teach you from the Word, expect to learn.

GUIDE TO STUDY 6

DAY 1 a) Which of them was the greatest, or most important?
b) Examples might come from world leaders, sportsmen, Christian leaders, musicians, etc.

DAY 2 a) Various suggestions may be given: e.g. dependence on His Father, imperfection with a willingness to learn, simplicity, ready acceptance of others.
b) They would have to change their whole outlook. (Most versions say 'changed'. AV 'be converted' must be taken literally as 'be turned around').

DAY 3 a) Jesus is concerned for every individual, 'one of these little ones', that they should come to know Him; and His anger is on anyone who commits the fearful sin of standing between another and Him.
b) Personal.

DAY 4 a) Suggestions may include poor people, handicapped, people who seem to be good at nothing, another race, etc.
b) The story of the lost sheep shows that Jesus (The Shepherd) will go to great lengths to save even one sinner, as, in fact, He did when He gave His life on the cross.

DAY 5 a) To win that other person back into fellowship again.
b) Yes, they should be followed today, in love.
c) Personal.

DAY 6 a) Names of specific people.
b) Attitude of forgiveness.

DAY 7 a) Everyone has a huge 'debt' of sin before God. One can only be forgiven by accepting Christ, who has paid that debt, therefore the ones whom the King forgives now belong to His Kingdom.
b) Personal.

GUIDE TO STUDY 7

(Bring a map to your study time). From Galilee to Judea, Jesus crossed the river Jordan, crossed back and then travelled through Jericho up to Jerusalem.

DAY 1   a) His imminent death by crucifixion.
b) Concerned at their need, and willing to heal.

DAY 2   a) When God joins two people in marriage, they are united and are to remain as one.
b) Yes. (Prepare for some discussion).

DAY 3   a) Because His disciples tried to discourage the people from bringing their children to Him (LB 'shooed them away!').
b) Because of Jesus' recent illustration with the child, which we read last week.
c) Jesus was showing that people who had the childlike qualities of trust, openness and receptiveness to Him were the ones who would respond to Him.

DAY 4   a) Trust in his own wealth preventing him from following Jesus.
b) He loved him.
c) Lessons – Jesus sees to the root of the problem; it is important to keep the commandments, but this is not enough; it is hard for rich people to enter the Kingdom.

DAY 5   a) 'With man this is impossible, but with God, all things are possible.'
b) That they would reign and rule over Israel in the New Age and receive a hundred times more of everything they had given up for Christ's sake; and eternal life.

DAY 6   a) He is Sovereign, and does what He knows is best. He is perfectly just.
b) Personal.

DAY 7   a) She believed that Jesus would be King in the Kingdom of Heaven. She was ambitious for her sons.
b) If someone wants to be great, he must to be servant of all. Examples such as: a missionary sacrificing ease and comfort to work among primitive people; someone giving up a lucrative job to do what God has called him to; anyone who puts the good of others before his own desires.

MATTHEW • ANSWER GUIDE

GUIDE TO STUDY 8

DAY 1 a) The large crowds who followed Jesus (presumably from Jericho) spread their cloaks on the road and cut branches and spread them on the road. They shouted 'Hosanna' and a verse from Psalm 118. They knew who Jesus was.
b) The people of Jerusalem did not know Jesus, and they were stirred (shaken, in an uproar) at His triumphal entry.
c) Jesus knew He would soon lay down His life for mankind and it was fitting that everyone should know of His presence in the city.
In fulfilling Zechariah's prophecy, He was identifying with Zion's promised King. Also, He perhaps wanted to give His followers an opportunity to demonstrate their loyalty.

DAY 2 a) Jesus. Driving out the money-changers and traders because they were making God's house into a den of robbers.
b) The blind and the lame.
c) They were shouting, 'Hosanna to the Son of David!'

DAY 3 a) They did not believe that Jesus was the Son of God.
b) Because they would not have believed Him.

DAY 4 a) The tax collectors and prostitutes, because they had been sinful, but had changed when they came into the Kingdom.
b) The chief priests and the elders because they appeared to be doing the will of God, but in fact did not do it.

DAY 5 a) The Jewish nation.
b) The owner – God; The tenants – the chief priests and elders; The servants – The prophets; The son – Jesus.

DAY 6 a) Personal.
b) Personal.

DAY 7 a) They refused to come.
b) Some ignored His servants. Others seized and killed them.
c) The wedding clothes represent Christ's robe of righteousness.

GUIDE TO STUDY 9

DAY 1
a) 1. When the temple would be destroyed.
2. What the sign would be of Jesus' coming. (The disciples probably expected Him to come in judgment while He was still in the flesh, as His death and resurrection had no meaning for them at this time – see Luke 9:45).
3. When the 'End of the Age' would be.
b) Watch out that no-one deceives you.

DAY 2
a) Wars and rumours of wars; Famines; Earthquakes; Persecution of Christians; A turning away from the faith; False prophets; Increase in wickedness.
b) Chapter 23:38 and chapter 24:2.

DAY 3
a) No-one knows the day or hour when He will return, and there will be no warning.
b) Personal.

DAY 4
a) The one 'in charge' had to give food to the others and care for them
b) As Galatians 6:10 says, our attitude should be that of caring for others, as we wait for Jesus' return.

DAY 5
a) The wise virgins made sure they were prepared, ready for His return.
b) We too, should see to it that we are ready if Jesus should return today.

DAY 6
a) In each there is an absent Lord; people with a certain relationship to him expecting him to return some time, but not knowing when; and the contrast between those who were doing his will in his absence, and those who were not.
b) Their faithfulness.

DAY 7
a) Personal.
b) Personal.

GUIDE TO STUDY 10

DAY 1   a) With all the darkness of sin and Satan closing in around Him, this must have been a ray of light to His soul. She poured some expensive perfume over Him.

b) Various suggestions may be given, e.g. Keeping in touch and talking to Him often; Listening to Him speaking through His word; Praising Him with others; Doing loving acts to others for His sake.

DAY 2   a) He betrayed Him.

b) Seeing Jesus condemned.

DAY 3   a) He was fiercely loyal to Him.

b) Trying to defend Jesus with a sword and denying Him.

c) Because he was doing everything in his own strength and acting on impulses.

DAY 4   a) To find false evidence against Jesus so that they could put Him to death.

b) He was biased, dishonest and an unbeliever.

c) He didn't want to believe Jesus, because Jesus did not fit in with his preconceived ideas of what Christ would be like.

DAY 5   a) Are you the King of the Jews?

b) He made a feeble effort to release Jesus, but allowed the crowd to choose Barabbas; His wife told him of her warning in a dream; He symbolically washed his hands of the responsibility.

DAY 6   a) They had heard that He claimed to be a King.

b) Quiet, dignified, brave, strong.

DAY 7   a) God's plan for Him had been written there, and He knew He was now fulfilling that plan.

b) It can show us how God wants us to live; Be a comfort in times of sorrow; Give us His promises (2 Tim. 3:16).

GUIDE TO STUDY 11

DAY 1
a) That he claimed to be King of the Jews.
b) They mocked Him about it (v. 42).

DAY 2
a) 'God was powerless to help this man, which proves that He can't be the Son of God.'
b) God's perfect plan of atonement for sinful man was being worked out, and Jesus had to die. If He had saved Himself at this point, He couldn't have saved us.

DAY 3
Midday darkness for three hours.
The curtain in the Temple torn from the top.
Earthquake.
Dead bodies raised to life.

DAY 4
a) The Centurion.
Many women.
Joseph of Arimathea.
b) They thought the disciples might steal the body and pretend He had risen as He said.

DAY 5
a) They were terrified, shook with fear, and fell down as dead men.
b) 'Go and tell my brothers to meet me in Galilee.'

DAY 6
a) Because no-one would ever find the dead body of Jesus.
b) Personal.

DAY 7
Personal.

THE WORD WORLDWIDE

We first heard of WORD WORLDWIDE over twenty years ago when Marie Dinnen, its founder, shared excitedly about the wonderful way ministry to one needy woman had exploded to touch many lives. It was great to see the Word of God being made central in the lives of thousands of men and women, then to witness the life-changing results of them applying the Word to their circumstances. Over the years the vision for WORD WORLDWIDE has not dimmed in the hearts of those who are involved in this ministry. God is still at work through His Word and in today's self-seeking society, the Word is even more relevant to those who desire true meaning and purpose in life. WORD WORLDWIDE is a ministry of WEC International, an interdenominational missionary society, whose sole purpose is to see Christ known, loved and worshipped by all, particularly those who have yet to hear of His wonderful name. This ministry is a vital part of our work and we warmly recommend the WORD WORLDWIDE 'Geared for Growth' Bible studies to you. We know that as you study His Word you will be enriched in your personal walk with Christ. It is our hope that as you are blessed through these studies, you will find opportunities to help others discover a personal relationship with Jesus. As a mission we would encourage you to work with us to make Christ known to the ends of the earth.

Stewart and Jean Moulds – British Directors, **WEC International.**

A full list of over 50 'Geared for Growth' studies can be obtained from:

John and Ann Edwards
5 Louvaine Terrace, Hetton-le-Hole, Tyne & Wear, DH5 9PP
Tel. 0191 5262803 Email: rhysjohn.edwards@virgin.net

Anne Jenkins
2 Windermere Road, Carnforth, Lancs., LA5 9AR
Tel. 01524 734797 Email: anne@jenkins.abelgratis.com

UK Website: www.gearedforgrowth.co.uk

2nd May.
my House.

Christian Focus Publications
publishes books for all ages

Our mission statement –

STAYING FAITHFUL

In dependence upon God we seek to help make His infallible word, the Bible, relevant. Our aim is to ensure that the Lord Jesus Christ is presented as the only hope to obtain forgiveness of sin, live a useful life and look forward to heaven with Him.

REACHING OUT

Christ's last command requires us to reach out to our world with His gospel. We seek to help fulfil that by publishing books that point people towards Jesus and help them develop a Christ-like maturity. We aim to equip all levels of readers for life, work, ministry and mission.

Books in our adult range are published in three imprints.

Christian Focus contains popular works including biographies, commentaries, basic doctrine, and Christian living. Our children's books are also published in this imprint.

Mentor focuses on books written at a level suitable for Bible College and seminary students, pastors, and other serious readers; the imprint includes commentaries, doctrinal studies, examination of current issues, and church history.

Christian Heritage contains classic writings from the past.

For details of our titles visit us on our website
www.christianfocus.com

Christian Focus Publications Ltd
Geanies House, Fearn, Tain,
Ross-shire, IV20 ITW, Scotland, United Kingdom.
info@christianfocus.com